Mel Bay Presents

Wedding Music For Two Violins

By Scott Staidle

Second Violin

Visit us on the Web at http://www.melbay.com — E-mail us at email@melbay.com

Table of Contents

This page has been left blank to avoid awkward page turns.

Air in "D"

for two violins

J. S. Bach
arr. Scott Staidle

Violin 2

Amazing Grace

for two violins

Traditional
arr. Scott Staidle

Violin 2

Allegro
for two violins

Fiocco
arr. Scott Staidle

Violin 2

arr. Scott Staidle

Violin 2

Menuetto

for two violins

Violin 2

Boccherini
arr. Scott Staidle

Jesu, Joy Of Man's Desiring

for two violins

J. S. Bach
arr. Scott Staidle

Violin 2

9

Kanon

for two violins

Pachelbel
arr. Scott Staidle

Violin 2

Violin 2

rall.

Ode to Joy

for two violins

L. van Beethoven
arr. Scott Staidle

Violin 2

Moderato

This page has been left blank to avoid awkward page turns.

Violin 2

Rondeau

for two violins

Mouret
arr. Scott Staidle

arr. Scott Staidle

Violin 2

Trumpet Voluntary

for two violins

Violin 2

Purcell
arr. Scott Staidle

Violin 2

Serenade

for two violins

J. Haydn
arr. Scott Staidle

Violin 2

Violin 2

Water Music/Hornpipe

for two violins

F. Handel
arr. Scott Staidle

Violin 2

Violin 2

Wedding March

for two violins

F. Mendelssohn
arr. Scott Staidle

Violin 2

Winter Mov. 2

for two violins

Violin 2

Vivaldi
arr. Scott Staidle

Bridal Chorus

for two violins

R. Wagner
arr. Scott Staidle

Violin 2

24

Mel Bay Presents

Wedding Music For Two Violins

By Scott Staidle

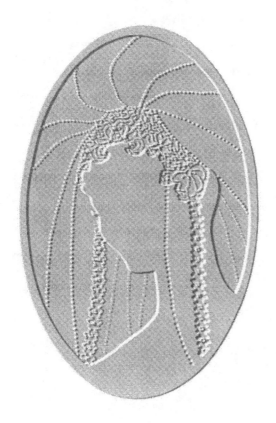

First Violin

Visit us on the Web at http://www.melbay.com — E-mail us at email@melbay.com

1 2 3 4 5 6 7 8 9 0

Table of Contents

About the Author

Scott Staidle, classical, rock and blues violinist, has been in the Louisville Orchestra since 1980. He has arranged music for violin duets, guitar & violin duets, string quartets and symphony orchestras. He has also played violin and guitar with rock, country and blues bands and is the founder of Derby City Strings. He can be contacted at:

cooltunes@ntr.net

Air in "D"

for two violins

J. S. Bach
arr. Scott Staidle

Violin 1

4

Amazing Grace

for two violins

Traditional
arr. Scott Staidle

Violin 1

Allegro

for two violins

Fiocco
arr. Scott Staidle

Violin 1

Violin 1

Violin 1

Menuetto

for two violins

Boccherini
arr. Scott Staidle

Jesu, Joy Of Man's Desiring

for two violins

J. S. Bach
arr. Scott Staidle

Violin 1

Kanon

for two violins

Pachelbel
arr. Scott Staidle

Violin 1

Violin 1

rall.

Ode to Joy

for two violins

L. van Beethoven
arr. Scott Staidle

Violin 1

This page has been left blank to avoid awkward page turns.

Rondeau

for two violins

Mouret
arr. Scott Staidle

Violin 1

Violin 1

Trumpet Voluntary

for two violins

Purcell
arr. Scott Staidle

Violin 1

Violin 1

rall.

Serenade

for two violins

J. Haydn
arr. Scott Staidle

Violin 1

Andante cantabile

Violin 1

Water Music/Hornpipe

for two violins

F. Handel
arr. Scott Staidle

Violin 1

Violin 1

Wedding March

for two violins

F. Mendelssohn
arr. Scott Staidle

Violin 1

Allegro mod.

mf   cresc.

f

Fine

mf

cresc.

f

D.S. al Fine

Winter Mov. 2

for two violins

Violin 1

Vivaldi
arr. Scott Staidle

Bridal Chorus

for two violins

R. Wagner
arr. Scott Staidle

Violin 1